The Children of the
SIERRA MADRE

THE WORLD'S CHILDREN

The Children of the
SIERRA MADRE

written and photographed by
FRANK STAUB

Carolrhoda Books, Inc./Minneapolis

Special thanks to Shelby Tisdale, anthropologist

Text and photographs copyright © 1996 by Frank Staub
Illustration copyright © 1996 by Carolrhoda Books, Inc.

This book is available in two editions:
Library binding by Carolrhoda Books, Inc.
Soft cover by First Avenue Editions
c / o The Lerner Group
241 First Avenue North
Minneapolis, MN 55401

LIBRARY OF CONGRESS CATALOGING-IN-PUBLICATION DATA

Staub, Frank J.
  The Children of the Sierra Madre / Frank Staub.
    p. cm. — (The world's children)
  Summary: Describes life in the Sierra Madre Occidental Mountains,
with a focus on the customs of the Tarahumara Indians.
  ISBN 0-87614-943-3 (lib. bdg.)
  ISBN 0-87614-967-0 (pbk.)
  1. Sierra Madre Occidental Region (Mexico)—Social life and
customs—Juvenile literature. 2. Children—Mexico—Sierra Madre
Occidental Region—Social life and customs—Juvenile literature.
3. Tarahumara Indians—Mexico—Sierra Madre Occidental Region—
Social life and customs—Juvenile literature. [1. Sierra Madre Occidental
Region (Mexico)—Social life and customs. 2. Tarahumara Indians.
3. Indians of Mexico—Mexico—Sierra Madre Occidental Region.]
I. Title. II. Series: World's children (Minneapolis, Minn.)
F1340.S73 1996
972–dc20   95-14543
                                                              CIP
                                                               AC

Manufactured in the United States of America
1 2 3 4 5 6 – JR – 01 00 99 98 97 96

Below: *Jesús and Javier with their teacher, Manuel Dominguez, in the shade of the old Satevó Mission Church*

Above: *The Sierra Madre Occidental is Mexico's largest mountain range. These mountains are higher than the Sierra Madre Oriental to the east and the Sierra Madre del Sur to the south. "Sierra Madre" means "mother mountain" in Spanish, the language of Mexico.*

Along the western edge of Mexico stretches a rugged chain of mountains called the Sierra Madre Occidental. Tucked into the rough peaks of these mountains is a series of beautiful, deep canyons. This area, located in the state of Chihuahua, is called Barrancas del Cobre, or Copper Canyon. It is home to many of the children of the Sierra Madre.

Even in mid-December, the weather in Barrancas del Cobre can be warm enough for Jesús and Javier's teacher to hold class outside. Their classroom lies in the shade of the old Satevó Mission Church at the bottom of Batopilas Canyon, part of Barrancas del Cobre.

Batopilas Canyon, or Barranca Batopilas, is deeper than the Grand Canyon. In fact, the canyons in Barrancas del Cobre are among the world's deepest. In some places, the canyons' top edges, or rims, are over a mile above the canyon bottoms.

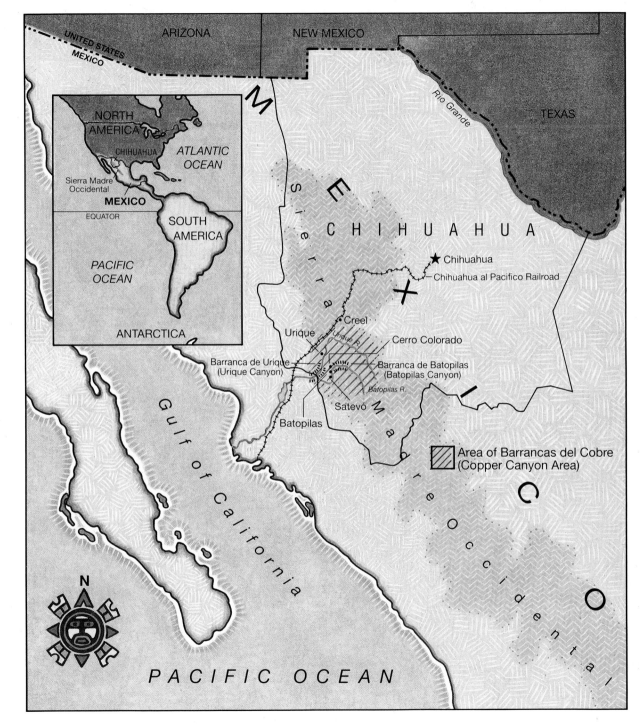

The tiny village of Satevó and the Satevó Mission sit beside the Batopilas River, which cuts Barranca Batopilas out of solid rock. No one knows why such a huge church was built in a place where so few people live. The road to Satevó was not even constructed until the late 1980s.

Over the years, the number of students in Jesús and Javier's school has grown. Some of the children live with their families in the tiny village of Satevó. The rest of the students walk down to school from small ranches, or ranchos, in the hills. Like most people in Mexico, these children are mestizos. Mestizos have some Indian ancestors and some ancestors from Spain. A small number of white Mexicans, who have no Indian heritage, also live in the Sierra Madre.

Like most Mexicans, these children from Satevó are mestizo, part Indian and part Spanish.

Many of Jesús and Javier's classmates live in houses like these.

9

The copper-colored Barrancas del Cobre is the largest system of canyons in North America. The high ridges and deep canyons make traveling difficult.

Spaniards first came to the Sierra Madre in the early 1600s. They mined gold, silver, and some copper, which may be how Copper Canyon got its name. "Barrancas del Cobre" may also refer to the copper color of some of the canyon walls.

Some of the early Spaniards were Catholic missionaries. They wanted to convert the local Indians to Christianity. Most of the Indians they met in the Sierra Madre were Tarahumara. About 50,000 Tarahumara now live in Barrancas del Cobre and the surrounding area. This part of the Sierra Madre is often called the Sierra Tarahumara.

The Tarahumara are a farming people, but the Spaniards forced many of them to work in the mines for little or no money. Many Tarahumara rebelled and many were killed. To make things worse, Spanish farmers took the Tarahumara's best farmland. Even after Mexico won its independence from Spain in 1821, the Tarahumara still had to plant their crops on the steepest slopes and in the rockiest canyons of the Sierra Madre. Even now, most Tarahumara farms are far from the main towns and roads.

A Tarahumara Indian boy

A Tarahumara farm in the mountains

11

Many mestizo and white Mexicans have moved to the Sierra Madre over the years, and they now outnumber the Indians by more than three to one. Most mestizos and whites live in towns, but many work on farms and ranches. Others are loggers, store owners, and construction workers, and a few still find enough gold to make a living as miners.

The Tarahumara generally get along with the other people who live in Barrancas del Cobre. Some Tarahumara have become part of the larger Mexican society. Still, many Mexicans look down on the Tarahumara. And many Tarahumara want to live apart from Mexicans, whom they think of as intruders in their land. The Tarahumara who live in separate communities have kept more of their traditions than almost any other group of native North Americans. Most still speak their native language, Rarámuri, in addition to Spanish. Many still wear traditional clothing—triangular waist cloths for men, and long, full skirts for women. Both men and women wear bright colors.

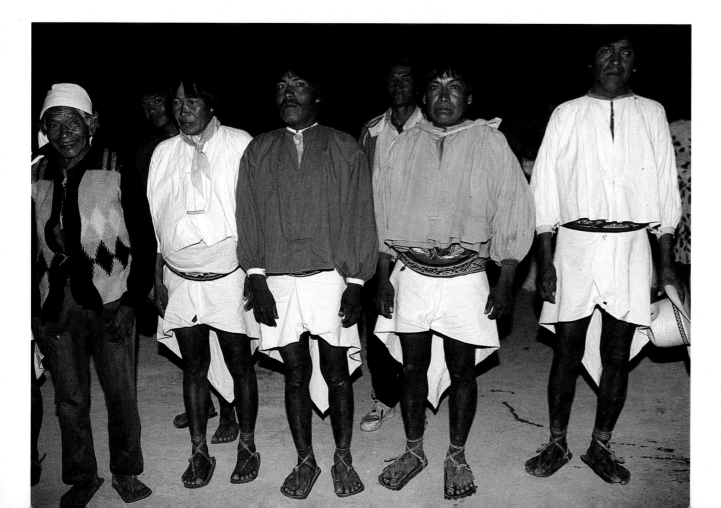

The Tarahumara resist attempts to make them part of modern Mexican society. They do not want to be told how to live.

Above: *Tarahumara girls wearing huarache sandals made from leather strips and old tire tread.*

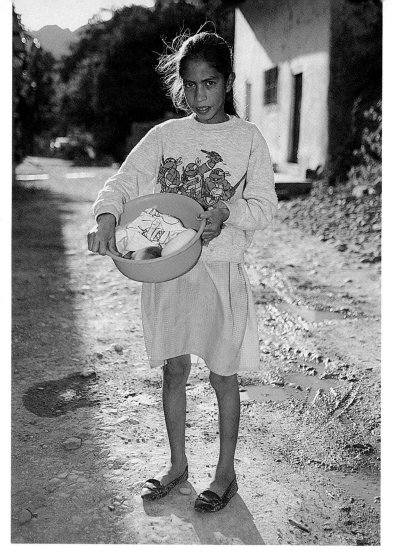

Selling bread and other homemade foods is one of the ways mestizo families make money in Batopilas.

More and more Tarahumara men are wearing modern clothing, like Patricio's white cowboy hat. Patricio sometimes does temporary work, such as digging ditches for underground water lines. Jobs like Patricio's are often the only contact many Tarahumara have with non-Indians. The Tarahumara often can't grow enough food on their rocky farmland, especially in years of low rainfall. During hard times, many Tarahumara work for mestizos in order to buy food. These jobs are usually low paying.

Patricio works in the town of Batopilas, where Satevó's schoolteacher, Manuel, lives. Monday through Friday, Manuel walks five miles down Batopilas Canyon to Satevó. Once a wealthy mining town, Batopilas is much larger than Satevó.

Patricio works in Batopilas.

The 94-mile bus ride from the canyon rim to Batopilas, at the bottom of the canyon, takes six hours along a steep, winding road.

15

Juan and his friends play marbles.

Batopilas has no movie theater and it is too far from a big city to get any television stations. This is not a problem for Juan and his friends, who entertain themselves by playing marbles after school. Juan has lighter skin and hair than his mestizo friends because most of his ancestors are from Europe.

Although some of the people living in Batopilas are white and some are Tarahumara, most are mestizo like Erica, Maria, and Christina.

They like to play *ali laga,* a game similar to jump rope.

Rita and her sisters, Janet and Claudia, often wait for their father to walk home after a hard day of work. He farms their family's land in the hills above town.

Mestizo farmers in Barrancas del Cobre usually grow corn, which they dry and grind into flour for traditional Mexican foods, such as tortillas and tamales. Beans are another important crop for mestizo farmers.

Christina and Maria hold the rope while Erica jumps, in a game of ali laga.

While Rita sits with her sisters, their brother Manola (on right) plays in the Batopilas River next to town. Many of the people of Batopilas use the river for bathing, doing laundry, and washing their horses.

Benito goes to a Catholic school in Batopilas. Ever since the Spaniards brought Catholicism to Mexico, it has been an important part of Mexican culture.

One of Mexico's most important religious holidays is the Fiesta of the Virgin of Guadalupe on December 12. It honors the day in 1531 when the Virgin Mary, Jesus's mother, is believed to have appeared to a poor Aztec Indian named Juan Diego, near Mexico City. The people in Batopilas celebrate the event by following a truck carrying the Virgin's picture. At certain points along the route, a woman dressed like Mary stands on a rock or hillside above the crowd, and the procession stops to pray. The procession ends at a shrine of the Virgin Mary on the edge of town.

Above: The nuns who teach at Benito's school are strict. Benito was late to class today, so he must do his assignment in the doorway. Right: A nun and a group of children in Batopilas wait for the Virgin of Guadalupe procession to begin.

A woman dressed like Mary stands above the crowd.

A band plays as the Virgin of Guadalupe procession winds through the center of Batopilas.

Many Tarahumara have accepted the Christian religion as their own.

Many Tarahumara have combined Catholicism with their traditional religious beliefs. They believe the Christian god is the same as their god, called Onorúame (Great Father) or Repa Beteame (He Who Lives Above). Religious rituals and celebrations are an important part of Tarahumara culture. The Tarahumara often play music and dance through the night on holidays such as Christmas and the Fiesta of the Virgin of Guadalupe.

One special celebration for many Tarahumara occurs during the week before Easter, called Holy Week, or Semana Santa in Spanish. Semana Santa is one of the few times when many Tarahumara come down into town. They gather at the Catholic churches to celebrate. Although Semana Santa is a Christian event, the Tarahumara have combined it with their own traditions, including drum ceremonies and colorful costumes. The Tarahumara and mestizos usually have separate celebrations for these Christian holidays.

Rosalba is 18 years old and has a baby daughter named Teresa. Tarahumara often get married and start having children while they are still teenagers. Tarahumara mothers hold their babies or carry them in special cloths against their bodies almost all the time. Unfortunately, not all Tarahumara children make it through childhood. Some children die from diseases such as measles and tuberculosis or from illnesses they catch from drinking dirty water.

Tarahumara children are usually allowed a great deal of freedom and responsibility. When boys and girls are very young, they learn to take care of the farm animals, make clothing, and cook. When they get older, these jobs are usually done by the girls, while boys learn how to use an ax, raise crops, hunt, and build things. But if a Tarahumara man's wife gets sick, he can do the housework because he learned how to do it as a child.

Left: *Rosalba with her baby daughter, Teresa, and Rosalba's sister.* Opposite page: *Tarahumara children wait for a store to open.*

Above: *Maria watches her family's goats, while her mother, Fermina, sits by the house.*

Looking after the farm animals is one of a Tarahumara child's most important jobs. Maria must keep her family's goats from wandering off and getting into the crops. Sometimes she must move them far from the house so they can find enough plants to eat.

The Tarahumara usually do not kill their farm animals, unless they want meat for an important feast or if their crops fail. But without farm animals, they might not have much to eat at all, because they use animal manure to fertilize their crops. Manure contains nutrients that plants need to grow, and much of the soil in the Sierra Madre needs nutrients. A Tarahumara farmer may move the family animals around the field every few days before planting crops. This fertilizes the entire field with nutrient-rich manure.

Above: *Many fields in the Sierra Madre are too rocky for crops, but they are useful for grazing animals.* Right: *Animals are important to most people in the Sierra Madre.*

A mother and daughter use their burro to help carry a heavy load.

According to the Tarahumara custom of *korima,* you must give food to those that ask for it. Tarahumara families that raise more than enough food often give to those in need. This sharing of food is important in times of hardship.

Tarahumara families often live miles apart, but they get together to share the work of planting and harvesting their crops and to have parties called *tesgüinadas.* At a *tesgüinada,* the adults drink beer called *tesgüino* that is made from corn and contains a small amount of alcohol. *Tesgüinadas* are held during religious festivals and at other times throughout the year.

Tarahumara families often help each other by sharing their farm animals. A family without burros or oxen might borrow animals from a neighbor to help plow their fields.

The Tarahumara have a simple but healthy diet. They grow corn, beans, squash, wheat, potatoes, and fruits. Malacio, Roberto, and Luis help their family by catching fish. They also enjoy spending time by a creek on a sunny day.

Many Tarahumara are expert hunters. They hunt wild turkeys, rabbits, squirrels, otters, badgers, skunks, raccoons, opossums, foxes, and other animals. Traps, bows and arrows, spears, rocks, and guns help them catch their prey. Sometimes they hunt with only their hands. But as more and more people come to the Sierra Madre and destroy the places where the animals live, there are fewer animals to hunt. The Mexican grizzly and the imperial woodpecker have already disappeared. While it lived, the imperial woodpecker was the world's largest woodpecker.

A Tarahumara girl eats an apple.

Roberto's fishing pole is long so he can place the hook right where he sees a fish. His brothers Malacio and Luis watch.

Moises hauls adobe bricks on the backs of his burros. The bricks were made from mud along the Batopilas River. Adobe bricks can be used in building houses or other buildings. Moises and his burros must travel up a steep mountain trail. Walking in the Sierra Madre can often be difficult, even with burros to carry the load. On this trip, Moises cut his ankle on a rock.

Moises and other Mexicans often ride their horses and mules, but the Tarahumara generally walk. Before Europeans brought horses to North America, most people traveled on foot. The Tarahumara still use leg power—many of the slopes around their homes and farms are too steep for even a mule. Walking or running is often the only way to cross this rugged land.

Below: *Two mestizo boys cross the Urique River on a mule.*

Above: *Horse washing in the Batopilas River*

Most Tarahumara walk when traveling across the rugged Sierra Madre. This family crosses the Batopilas River.

Rodrigo

To save time when traveling from place to place, Rodrigo and many other Tarahumara often run. In fact, the Tarahumara have been called the world's greatest natural runners. The word Tarahumara comes from *rarámuri,* their word meaning "the foot runners." Rarámuri is also the name of their language.

Sometimes Rodrigo competes in team races in the mountains. Each team has a small wooden ball that team members kick as they run through hills and canyons. The first team to get its ball across the finish line wins. These races may be anywhere from 10 to over 100 miles long. Racers sometimes carry flashlights or torches as they run through the night.

Below: *Antonio and Margarita at their cave house just below the canyon rim.*

Antonio and Margarita's family lives in a house at the mouth of a shallow cave. Their cave stays nice and cool in the summer. It's dark inside, but they do most of their cooking, working, and playing outside, since the skies in the Sierra Madre are usually clear with plenty of sunshine. Most Tarahumara live in houses made of wood, stone, or adobe bricks with very little furniture.

Antonio and Margarita's cave house is near the rim of Urique Canyon. During the winter, the temperature at night can dip below freezing. Some Tarahumara families who live on the canyon rim move to warmer canyon bottoms for the winter. But Antonio and Margarita's family stays here all year long. With the help of a fire, their cozy cave house warms up quickly on cold winter mornings.

Tarahumara houses and storage buildings are simple but sturdy.

Canuto fixes a dam with rocks and branches. Getting clean water is often a problem in the Sierra Madre.

The mestizos and whites in the Sierra Madre spend more time indoors than the Tarahumara do. Their homes usually have tables, chairs, beds, stoves, and floors of wood or concrete. But they, too, depend on their natural environment. Their drinking water, for example, often comes from streams and rivers. Several miles from Batopilas, Canuto fixes a dam that holds water for his hometown of Cerro Colorado.

Canuto's son Alfredo has just left Cerro Colorado to guide a group of backpackers from the United States. When Alfredo was young, Canuto taught him how to be a guide. For this trip, Alfredo will take the group to the town of Urique, about 25 miles away at the bottom of the Urique Canyon. A burro carries some of their load. The backpackers have sleeping bags, tents, and expensive hiking boots. But Alfredo travels light—he wears sandals and sleeps outside beneath a single blanket.

Left and below left: *Alfredo and his burro lead a group of backpackers.*

Below: *The backpackers in camp*

The town of Urique has almost no traffic, so the children often play in the main street after school.

The backpackers hike the 25 miles to Urique in three days. Like most parts of Copper Canyon, Urique is isolated. The steep canyon road into town was not built until the 1970s.

The backpackers arrive during the Christmas season. As they walk down Urique's main street, they pass a store owned by Diego's family. The store is ready for Christmas, with plenty of gifts and decorations for sale.

Christmas is the time for *posadas* in Mexico. *Posada* means "inn" in Spanish. During a *posada*, Mexicans remember the night when Mary and Joseph, Jesus's parents, could not find a room at an inn. People light candles and walk from house to house, singing a song, asking for a place to stay.

Diego at his parents' store

Children in Urique light candles for a posada.

Above: *Vast evergreen forests surround Creel, and many people here work in the lumber industry. But more and more trees are being cut down. Only two percent of the original pine forest is left in the Sierra Madre Occidental. Many Tarahumara have fought against this logging.*

Right: *People started talking about building the Chihuahua al Pacifico Railroad in the 1870s, but it was not finished until 1961. Travelers from all over the world visit Mexico to ride this spectacular railroad.*

Creel, the largest town in Barrancas del Cobre, sits high in the mountains. It is much colder and wetter here than in the towns on the canyon bottoms. Creel is named after Enrique Creel, one of the powerful men who had a railroad built from the Pacific Ocean to the state of Chihuahua's capital city, also called Chihuahua. This railroad is called the Chihuahua al Pacifico Railroad. Laying track through the rugged Sierra Madre was difficult. The roughest part of the route has 37 bridges and 86 tunnels.

The railroad brings tourists through Creel to view the beautiful scenery of Copper Canyon. Tourists also come to buy Tarahumara crafts, such as the belts that Cuca and Maria's mother makes. Selling things for money is a newer part of Tarahumara culture. In the past, the Tarahumara traded things for what they could not grow or make, and helped those who did not have enough.

Cuca and her sister Maria make money for their family by selling belts in Creel. They use some of their money, though, to buy bubble gum.

41

Just outside of Creel, Maria Elena sits with her mother-in-law, Guadalupe, and Guadalupe's young son, Roberto. Guadalupe uses a loom to weave colorful belts like the ones Cuca and Maria sell.

Not far away, Crucita sells dolls that her mother made. When Crucita is not selling dolls or helping her family in some other way, she goes to the San Ignacio Mission school near Creel. The Mexican government wants all children to get an education. Many Tarahumara children do not go to school, though, because they live too far away.

Sabrina lives a long way from Creel. She does not go to school. But she is learning to make baskets from leaves of the agave plant. She cuts the tough leaves into long, thin strips and weaves the strips into the shape of a basket. Handmade baskets are one of the best-selling items for the tourists. The Tarahumara are world famous for their basket-making skills.

Above: *Crucita with dolls her mother made.* Opposite page: *Maria Elena and Roberto watch as Guadalupe makes belts.*

Below: *Sabrina holds a finished basket and the strips of agave leaves that she uses to make her baskets.*

A Tarahumara mother gazes into a shop window in Creel.

Tourists are not the only people coming to Barrancas del Cobre. Since 1900 the number of white and mestizo Mexicans living in the Copper Canyon area has doubled. New roads are appearing and more and more trees are being cut down for lumber. The beautiful scenery is changing.

More people in the region has meant a rise in crime and pollution. It has also become harder for the people of Barrancas del Cobre to hold on to their traditional ways of life. As the children of the Sierra Madre Occidental grow up, they will face challenges in their changing world.

Children from the smallest villages in Barrancas del Cobre now have contact with the outside world.

Children holding the Mexican flag.

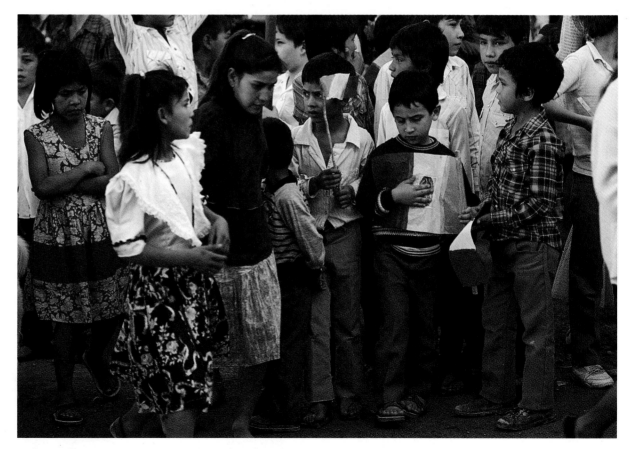

Pronunciation Guide

adobe ah-DOH-bay
ali laga AH-lee LAH-gah
Barrancas del Cobre bar-RAHN-kahs del KOH-bray
Batopilas bah-toh-PEE-lahs
Chihuahua chih-WAH-wah
huarache wah-RAH-chay
korima KOH-ree-mah
mestizo mes-TEE-zoh
Onorúame oh-nor-OO-ah-may
posada poh-SAH-dah
Rarámuri rah-RAH-moo-ree
Repa Beteame RAY-pah bay-TAY-ah-may
Satevó sah-tay-VOH
Sierra Madre Occidental see-AIR-rah MAH-dray
  ohk-see-den-TAHL
tamale tah-MAH-lay
Tarahumara tah-rah-oo-MAR-ah
tesgünada tehs-wee-NAH-dah
tesgüino tehs-WEE-noh
tortilla tor-TEE-yah
Urique oo-REE-kay

Index